MUSIC MINUS ONE PIANO

RAVEL

THE PIANO TRIO

MMO 3061

COMPACT DISC PAGE AND BAND INFORMATION

MMO CD 3061

Music Minus One

RAVEL
The Piano Trio
Piano

à André GEDALGE

TRIO

for Piano, Violin and 'Cello

Piano

I.

Maurice Ravel
(1875 - 1937)

8 taps (1 measure)
precede movement

II. __Pantoum

III. __Passacaille

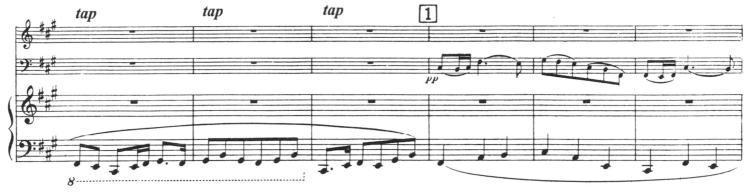

lV.___Final

October, 1991

MUSIC MINUS ONE PIANO

MMO 3061

RAVEL

THE PIANO TRIO

MUSIC MINUS ONE • 50 Executive Boulevard • Elmsford, New York 10523-1325
Tel: (914) 592-1188   Fax: (914) 592-3116
E-mail: mmomus@aol.com   Websites: www.minusone.com *and* www.pocketsongs.com